INNERACTIONS

INNERACTIONS

*Visions to Bring
Your Inner and Outer Worlds
into Harmony*

STEPHEN C. PAUL, PH.D.

with paintings by

GARY MAX COLLINS

HarperSanFrancisco
A Division of HarperCollins*Publishers*

FIRST EDITION

LIBRARY OF CONGRESS CATALOGING-IN-PUBLICATION DATA
Paul, Stephen C.
    Inneractions / Stephen C. Paul with paintings by Gary Max
Collins.
    —1st ed.
        p.   cm.
    ISBN 0-06-250711-7 (alk. paper)
    1. Self-actualization (Psychology)   2. Conduct of life.
    I. Collins, Gary.   II. Title.   III. Title: Inneractions.
BF637.S4P378   1992
158—dc20   91-58142
                                                               CIP

    93 94 95 96 ❖ HCP-HK 10 9 8 7 6 5 4 3 2

This book is dedicated

to those people

who are choosing

to bring their consciousness

with them

into the world.

After all of the changes you have made, you still wake up here every day. This book is for those of you who are beginning to live the life of your dreams, a life of greater inner peace and of greater fulfillment in the outside world. It is for those of you who are adding something positive to the earth by adding more of your Self.

Our first book, *Illuminations,* offered a challenge both to face denial and pretense and to take actions to bring your life more in line with who you truly are. *Inneractions* is a challenge to live life consciously and mindfully. The sayings reflect day-to-day choices and actions that can bring your inner life and the external world into harmony. They describe the practice of daily conscious living.

The term "inneractions" suggests actions that arise from within rather than those triggered in reaction to the external world. It recognizes the source within that perceives and chooses. It recognizes consciousness. Inneractions arise from awareness.

Gary's paintings are primarily inspired by nature. Nature restores us, instructs us, and shows us the divine in an approachable way. Through his collection of remarkably diverse images, Gary transports us to a succession of sacred sanctuaries and private retreats.

We hope these thoughts and images will remind you and inspire you as you walk solidly, but softly, upon this planet. May you walk mindfully, and may you walk in beauty and peace.

INNERACTIONS

No matter how evolved you become

you still wake up here every morning.

It's time

to make

your own dreams

come true.

Dream your dream, focus your intention,

and take each step to make it real.

Every step you take

should move you

in the direction

of your vision.

Press out

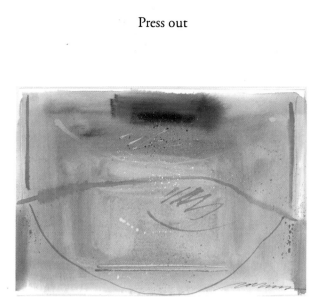

beyond

your imagined

limits.

The more free you are

from your ego

the more effortless

life becomes.

You can't

control outcomes

but you can dare

to pursue your desires.

The more

you let go

the more

you accomplish.

It's your turn

to make up

the meaning

of your life.

Acknowledge your natural gifts

and find ways to

fully express them.

Create the world

you dream of

with every choice

you make.

Take total

responsibility

for the fulfillment

of your vision.

Approach

your life

as an artist

creating.

If there's something to do, do it.

If not, relax and have fun.

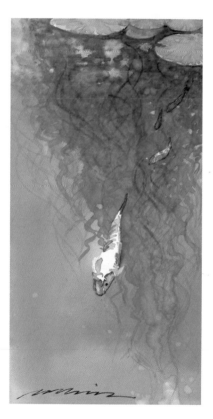

Whatever

you do,

do it

with reverence.

Soften the judgments

and sharp definitions

that keep you separate

from all that's around you.

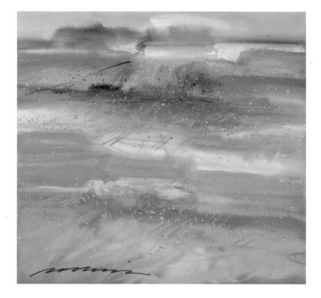

Give others the freedom

to be themselves.

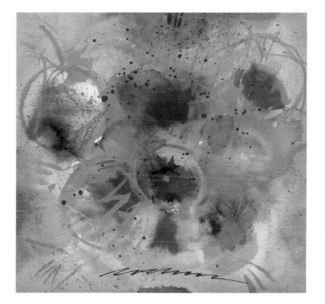

Look for companions who are willing

to search for themselves.

If you love someone,

listen very hard

to that person's unique

but equal truth.

Accept your

partner's limits,

and stay or go

based on your own.

Risk the truth

with those you love

and give them the gift

you would want for yourself.

The love of your life

will love and accept you,

share your adventures,

and show you your folly.

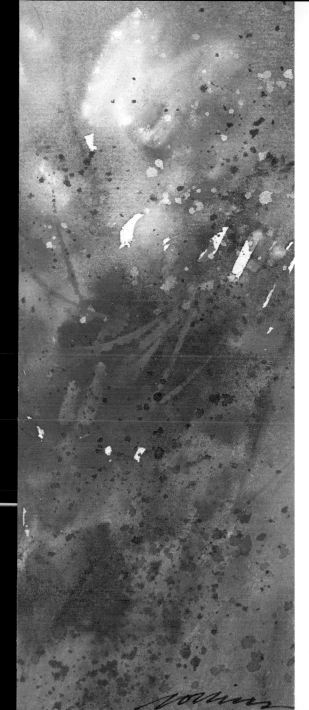

Never miss
a single chance
to express your love
spontaneously.

There are

countless ways

to express love.

Be creative!

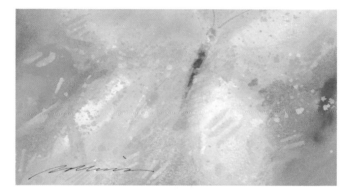

To keep romance alive

don't forget

the element

of surprise.

Making love

is a chance

to embrace

the divine.

Life is a series

of opportunities

to act more

consciously.

Slow down.

There's nothing

more precious

than now.

Begin to see

what *is* in front of you,

rather than

what you learned is there.

The place in which you find yourself

isn't nearly as important

as where you place your attention

while you are there.

To live

your life fully

you'll have to stay present

and face your experience.

Make the effort

to be conscious

of the motives

behind your actions.

You have

absolute freedom

to choose

in every instant.

Once you release
your expectations
about the future
there is only now.

You are the

conscious meeting

of heaven

and earth.

Your daily affairs are the sacred ceremonies

you perform within the temple of your life.

What are the steps

that you need to take

so your life will flow

more simply and effortlessly?

Take time to remember

what's important in your life.

Take time

to be alone

and

listen.

The destination

is "to be"

and not to arrive

somewhere else.

Reduce the distractions

in your life

and make room

for subtlety.

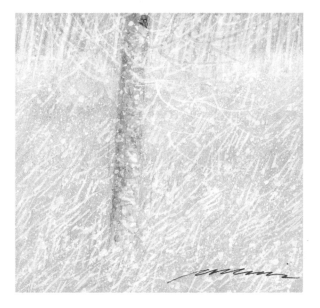

Pay attention

and you'll find

many perfect moments

in any given day.

Surround yourself with nature

and let it breathe life into your soul.

Create a home that welcomes you

at the end of every day.

Treat yourself

as an

honored guest

in your own home.

Surround yourself

with simplicity and beauty

to enhance your life

and inspire you.

Refresh yourself continually

by doing those things that you love.

Everything you do can be done better

from a place of relaxation.

Cultivate

a loving

relationship

with your body.

Excess in any form is a great distraction—

but a lousy substitute for true joy.

Cleanse and nourish

your whole being

by eating

consciously.

Celebrate your body

through movement and exercise—

keep it fit, energized,

and vital for a lifetime.

Remove the rock

from your shoe

rather than learn

to limp comfortably.

Always walk away

with your self-respect.

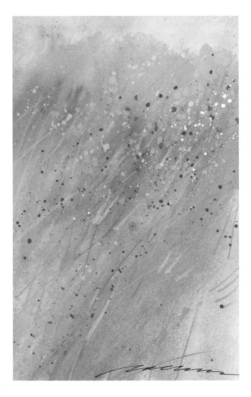

Free yourself

from the responsibility

of making

others happy.

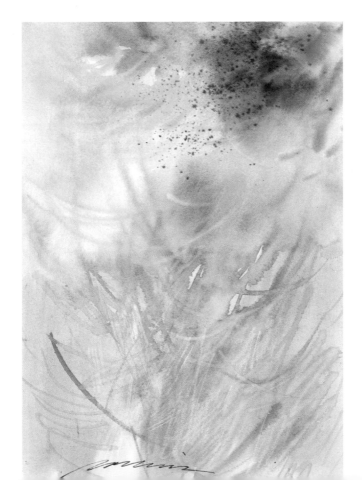

Avoid people

who still prefer

that you

pretend.

Always be willing

to recognize and accept

the truth in front of you

and base your actions on it.

Express yourself

honestly and directly

and let the cards

fall where they will.

Avoid saying yes when your answer

should be no.

There's no reason

to stay

where you don't

want to be.

When you let go of responsibility

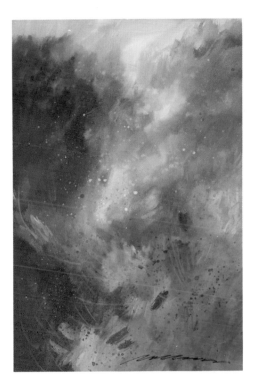

you can experience a taste of freedom.

How you

live your life

is your true

spiritual practice.

Once you discover

your own true self

you can find

your place in everything.

To become

a good person,

become

yourself.

To be yourself

will be more fun

than anything

you've ever done.

To live life

with integrity

requires that you never

forget who you are.

Strive for

complete congruence

between your inner

and outer lives.

Be sure there aren't

any parts of yourself

left in pockets of exception

outside your awareness.

Before you

speak or act

take time to find

your center.

Gladly greet

each of the

changing seasons

of your life.

The more spontaneous

you become

the more alive

you will feel.

Take time to complete

the needed changes

in your own life

before tackling the world.

Your laughter

will bring joy

back into

the world.

The whole world

is a gift

waiting for

your acceptance.

Expand your vision

until it includes

the whole earth

as your home.

Gracefully

dance with

the earth's

limitations.

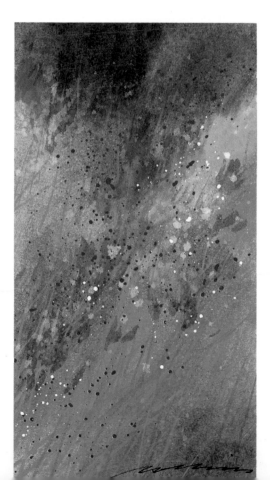

Catch the

rhythm

and join

the dance.

Take time to notice

how amazing

your world

truly is.

In a world

of appearances

be sure to weigh

the underlying substance.

Recognize and respect life

in its many forms.

Touch the earth

ever so gently

through each

of your senses.

Since nothing on earth

is inconsequential

use the resources you must

with grateful awareness.

Leave room

for

a little

magic.

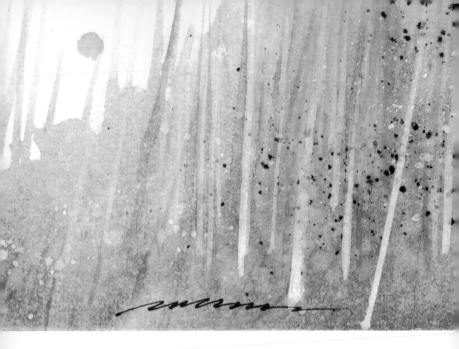

All it ever takes

to step from the ordinary

and into the magical

is your undivided attention.

One day you must

leap or fall

into the arms

of the universe.

If there is

a direction to go

it will flow over you

and direct you.

Life always tells you

if you're going in the right

or wrong direction

if only you listen.

Your eyes and ears can

guide you through the apparent,

but your feelings and intuition

must lead you through the mystery.

Always be ready

to take

the next clear step

you see.

Remember the feeling

of peace and joy

that comes

in the moment of oneness?

Ultimately

you will

have to

trust.

Today came much sooner

than you ever dreamed.

The future

won't match

your

illusions.

You can always open more,

and there's always more to open to.

Pass

through the door

when it

opens.

Show

God

a good

time.

Acknowledgments

We would like to thank Jackie Pratt for her
personal example, inspiration, practical guidance,
and constant support through the course of both
of our books. I personally would like to thank her
for being my loving teacher and companion. She
helped me with the vision and with following it
through.

John Collins has continually served as an
artistic sounding board, source of encouragement,
motivator, and reality checkpoint for Gary
through both monumental artistic undertakings.
He helped Gary through when the challenge
seemed overwhelming.

We both want to express our appreciation
to Barbara Moulton, our editor at Harper
San Francisco, for recognizing our work and for
her success in bringing it to you in such a beautiful
form.

About the Author

Stephen C. Paul, Ph.D., is a psychotherapist, educator, artist, and Tai Chi instructor based in Salt Lake City, Utah. He received his doctorate in clinical psychology from the University of Missouri and has taught and counseled at the University of Utah. His private practice focuses on brief, intensive work with people who are highly motivated to change.

About the Artist

Gary Collins's paintings are exhibited internationally. A native of Utah, he has been painting as far back as he can remember, with marked success since 1972. Before that he was a successful designer, businessman, and consultant. His crowning achievement, he says, is that his daughter and son are both successful artists as well.